A PLUME BOOK

DOES A BEAR SH*T IN THE WOODS?

CAROLINE TAGGART is the author of *I Used to Know That*, *A Classical Education*, *An Apple a Day*, and *Her Ladyship's Guide to the Queen's English*; coauthor of *My Grammar and I (or Should That Be "Me"?)*; and general editor of the *I Used to Know That* series.

does a bear sh*t in the woods?

Answers to Rhetorical Questions

caroline taggart

A PLUME BOOK

PLUME
Published by Penguin Group
Penguin Group (USA) Inc., 375 Hudson Street, New York, New York 10014,
U.S.A. • Penguin Group (Canada), 90 Eglinton Avenue East, Suite 700, Toronto,
Ontario, Canada M4P 2Y3 (a division of Pearson Penguin Canada Inc.) •
Penguin Books Ltd., 80 Strand, London WC2R 0RL, England • Penguin Ireland,
25 St. Stephen's Green, Dublin 2, Ireland (a division of Penguin Books Ltd.) • Penguin
Group (Australia), 250 Camberwell Road, Camberwell, Victoria 3124, Australia
(a division of Pearson Australia Group Pty. Ltd.) • Penguin Books India Pvt. Ltd.,
11 Community Centre, Panchsheel Park, New Delhi – 110017, India • Penguin Books
(NZ), 67 Apollo Drive, Rosedale, North Shore 0632, New Zealand (a division of
Pearson New Zealand Ltd.) • Penguin Books (South Africa) (Pty.) Ltd., 24 Sturdee
Avenue, Rosebank, Johannesburg 2196, South Africa

Penguin Books Ltd., Registered Offices: 80 Strand, London WC2R 0RL, England

Published by Plume, a member of Penguin Group (USA) Inc. Previously published
in the UK by Michael O'Mara Books as *Answers to Rhetorical Questions*.

First Plume Printing, August 2011
10 9 8 7 6 5 4 3

Ⓡ REGISTERED TRADEMARK—MARCA REGISTRADA

LIBRARY OF CONGRESS CATALOGING-IN-PUBLICATION DATA

Taggart, Caroline, 1954-
    Does a bear sh*t in the woods? : answers to rhetorical questions / Caroline
Taggart.
        p.   cm.
    "A Plume Book."
    ISBN 978-0-452-29707-4
    1. Questions and answers.   I. Title.   II. Title: Does a bear shit in the woods?
AG195.T252011
030—dc22   2010041911

Printed in the United States of America

CONTENTS

Acknowledgments   7

Introduction   9

1   **Where's the fire?**   11
    Questions of health, safety, and the law

2   **Do you know the way to San José?**   21
    Questions of geography, science, and nature

3   **Who wants to be a millionaire?**   43
    Questions of finance and business

4   **Is the Pope a Catholic?**   49
    Questions about the meaning of life

5   **Et tu, Brute?**   77
    Questions from literature, history, and politics

6   **Shall I compare thee to a summer's day?**   91
    Questions of social intercourse

7   **Does your mother know you're out?**   113
    Questions of domestic life

8   **Where's the beef?**   125
    Questions of food and drink

9   **Will you still love me tomorrow?**   135
    Questions of sex and romance

Afterword   159

ACKNOWLEDGMENTS

Many thanks to Anna and Toby, who knew what they wanted from this book and worked hard to help me achieve it; to Andrew for the cartoons and Glen for the design; to all the friends who contributed possible questions and even occasional answers; and to Ros for a ready supply of Scrabble and chocolate biscuits.

INTRODUCTION

Just in case you were wondering . . .

. . . a rhetorical question is a question that doesn't expect or require an answer, used for dramatic effect. Fowler's *Modern English Usage* elaborates by saying, "The assumption is that only one answer is possible and that if the hearer is impelled to make it mentally himself it will impress him more than the speaker's statement."

In other words, it is more effective to shrug your shoulders and ask, "Is the Pope a Catholic?" (forcing your hearer to think, "Yes, of course he is") than simply to say, "The Pope is a Catholic" (which your hearer almost certainly knows already).

Rhetorical questions are all around us, from the Bible ("Can the leopard change his spots?") to the popular song ("Who will buy this wonderful morning?"). A handful of them are deep and meaningful ("What does a woman want?"); many more are anxious ("Will you still love me tomorrow?") or frivolous ("Has your mother sold her mangle?"). What they have in common is that someone, somewhere, has thought them worth asking and—by definition—been left without a satisfactory response.

*Does a Bear Sh*t in the Woods?* attempts to deal with this problem in a sensible, no-nonsense way. After all, when it comes to the crunch, do you really *want* someone to compare you to a summer's day? How many beans do you *think* make five? Does your brother *need* a keeper?

The result is not the answer to questions of life, the universe, and everything. It's a potpourri of quotations from Shakespeare and the Marx Brothers, advertisements for burgers and slogans for political campaigns, lines from action films and titles of love songs. Something for everyone, you might say.

Or, to put it another way, what's not to like?

CHAPTER ONE

Where's the fire?

Questions of health, safety, and the law

What better way to begin than by establishing that we have filled in all the forms, ticked all the boxes, and ensured that no one is going to come to any harm?

Is your journey really necessary?

This one is between you and your conscience—and is probably the only question in the book of which that can be said. While we are encouraged to travel by bike or by public transport to save on fossil fuels, carbon emissions, and all the other evils attached to the private car, no one is (yet) officially saying that the planet would be a better place if we all stayed at home. But it can only be a matter of time.

Indeed, current estimates suggest that some 50 million US workers (or 40 percent of the employed population) could be based at home rather than the office for at least part of the working week. As yet, only about 2.5 million Americans call home their principal workplace, suggesting that a lot of commuting is unnecessary, assuming you're not worried about maintaining regular face-to-face contact with your professional associates.

Our other main reason for traveling is for leisure. A fulfilling leisure time is part of a balanced life and has many accepted benefits—improving physical and mental health, oiling the economy, developing personal relationships, increasing environmental awareness, bolstering community cohesion, developing personal leadership skills, and so on. If you give up any hobbies that involve a bit of travel, there may be a little less CO_2 in the air but society and you are likely to suffer in other ways. Home-based leisure activities such as Scrabble and crocheting are all very well, but they aren't going to do much for your leadership skills.

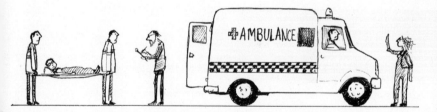

Am I my brother's keeper?

First of all, do you have a brother? If not, you might as well turn the page and read about something else. If you do, does he actually need keeping, or would you be better advised to let him get on with his life? Legally, you could conceivably become your brother's guardian (if not keeper) should he not yet be at the age of majority when he loses his parents or should he be physically or mentally unfit to look after himself. More improbably, you may also become your brother's keeper should he be the manager of a soccer or hockey team and decide to put you in goal.

Nonetheless, this is not a recommended retort when God asks where your brother is, especially if, like Cain, you've done away with him.

Do I feel lucky?

Only you can answer this question. So *do* you feel lucky? Or, as Clint Eastwood would put it, "Well, do ya, punk?" The punk in question didn't. He was. Moral: in counting the number of rounds someone has fired at you, it pays to be accurate.

Where's the fire?

Early fires were pretty random, relying as they did on lightning strikes, volcanoes, maybe the odd superheated meteorite, that sort of thing. Once Man got the hang of friction, though (useful in *so* many ways), he never looked back. Today your fire can be anywhere, provided you have equipped yourself with a means of ignition (matches, fire arrows, flamethrower) and some inflammable material (*clue*: gasoline-soaked straw, good; steel-reinforced concrete, less good; water, forget it). Otherwise, replying "In your eyes, you gorgeous beast!" when asked the question by a police patrolman who has pulled you over for speeding may not be the best idea you've had all day.

How many roads must a man walk down before you call him a man?

As many as he likes, as long as he doesn't ask for directions. Technically, if we accept that a child will begin walking at about a year old and becomes an adult at eighteen, and taking into account the 307 km (192 miles) an average person walks each year, we might come up with a figure of 5,222 km (3,264 miles). Which is probably quite a lot of roads, unless your road happens to be, say, the Pan-American Highway, when you will barely have covered a fifth of it.

However, as this is a chapter on health and safety, it should be pointed out that a man—or woman or child —should not be walking down a road at all; he should be walking on the pavement. Unless he is in the USA, that is, in which case the pavement is equally dangerous and the safer option is the sidewalk.

Guard

Guard's
guard

Guard's
guard's
guard

Guard's guard's
guard's
guard

Quis custodiet ipsos custodies?

This is Latin for "Who will guard the guards themselves?"
(first proposed in that language by Juvenal in his *Satires*)
and a mathematical paradox. If the guards have guards,
then who guards the guards' guards? Or, to put it another
way: "Big flea has little flea / Upon his back to biteum, /
Little flea has smaller flea, / And so *ad infinitum*." A
Christian might say that each guardian has, of course, a
guardian angel. But to be on the safe side, I'd advise that

the guards look after themselves, since they're so good at guarding.

This is, in fact, pretty much what Plato suggested in *The Republic* when pondering who should guard the City's guardians. He suggested telling the guardians a "noble lie," persuading them that, being superior to those they guard, it falls upon them to carry out their guardianship morally and fairly. That way, the guardians become self-guarding. One can but hope.

Cui bono?

Properly, *Cui bono est* [or *fuit*]?—literally, "To whom is [or was] it a benefit?" and normally translated as "Who profits by it?" The principle is often used by detectives (especially fictional ones), for if whoever profits from a crime can be established, there's a good chance that he or she is the criminal. It does not mean "What is Bono good for?" (properly, "What is the point of Bono?")—a question that none dare ask.

Can a man take fire in his bosom, and his clothes not be burned? Can one go upon hot coals and his feet not be burned?

It sounds unlikely, so let's consider the options.

A   Fire eaters in circuses swallow flaming torches for
a living and seem none the worse for it. However,
they only do this after extensive training and even
then use a special fire-eater's torch with purpose-
designed wicks and fuel. The classic pose to adopt
is with feet quite wide apart (for stability) and
head tilted back with mouth and nose pointed to
the sky. Then it's all about deep and controlled
breathing, which ensures the heat and flames
are kept safely away from the face. The mouth is
opened and the tongue comes out, flat and wide
in readiness for the torch, which is then taken into
the mouth. A final controlled puff of breath will
extinguish the torch at the end of the act.
Doesn't sound very sensible, does it? Best
avoided all around.

B   Self-help gurus say that walking on hot coals is a self-empowering motivational activity. But how is it done? Once coals have been burned, they are covered with ashes. Fire-walking is best done of an evening to give the coal time to reduce to slightly cooler embers (and because the evening light will make them look hotter than they are). Remembering that you have the evening air and a layer of ashes to act as a barrier between you and the coals, the trick is to walk across them without hesitating. It is not the walking that will burn you so much as the stopping. As per (a) above, I'm still not going to recommend it. If you need to boost your motivation, watching the *Rocky* movies is infinitely less dangerous.

C   Let me reiterate, I think they're crazy and these are just the sort of hazardous hobbies that play merry hell with your insurance premiums.

Your call.

CHAPTER TWO

Do you know the way to San José?

Questions of geography, science, and nature

When did we humans first start asking questions about our surroundings? And is there any subject so obscure or so mundane that we've haven't at some time pondered its meaning?

Is it me or is it hot in here?

If you are a woman aged between about forty-five and sixty, chances are it's you. You're having a hot flush. You'd think that all the hormonal changes that go on around this time would be enough for anyone to have to cope with, but no, the part of your brain that controls temperature is having its own private midlife crisis and giving you a great upper-body workout putting sweaters on and taking them off again. If you are one of the unlucky 10 percent, this could go on for fifteen years. I'd recommend sage tea, which is said to reduce sweating. In fact, it has multiple benefits—the ancient Egyptians used sage as a fertility drug, which may or may not be what you need at your time of life.

What is so rare as a day in June?

A day in April, September, or November is exactly as rare as a day in June (remember "Thirty days hath . . . "?). A day in February is rarer and February 29 rarest of all. But most days come around reliably every year, so there isn't really anything very rare about any of them.

How high the Moon?

A mean distance of 384,400 km (240,250 miles) above the Earth.

Where are the snows of yesteryear?

Melted, says Clever Britches. Not so, say scientists, who have studied core samples of ancient snow trapped as deep as 3,350 meters (11,000 feet) beneath the surface of the Antarctic ice sheets to garner information about the global climate over hundreds of thousands of years. There was, for instance, less CO_2 in the atmosphere 100,000 years ago, and much less radiation, nuclear testing being a relative newcomer in the scale of things. This is the sort of research that fires the syllabus of the University of the Blindingly Obvious. Still, it's nice to know that some of yesteryear's snows are still there in Antarctica, as well as many other areas of the world from Canada to Siberia to the top of Mount Kilimanjaro in Tanzania.

Actually, the fifteenth-century French poet François Villon, who first asked this question, was lamenting the passing of the heroic, virtuous, beautiful, etc., women of myth and history. Four centuries later, the English poet Dante Gabriel Rossetti found the translation so difficult that he had to invent the word "yesteryear," for which he is duly credited in dictionaries of the better sort.

Where have all the flowers gone?

There are numerous scenarios in which flowers might disappear, even over quite a large area (you could try Agent Orange, for one), but it is extremely unlikely that the world would be entirely deflowered. There are, as a best guest by experts, over 350,000 known flowering plants in the world and perhaps another 70,000 we have yet to discover. Not only do they stand around in flower beds or slightly questionable vases looking decorative, but they turn up on trees and bushes, cacti, waterlilies, all sorts of places—and they're persistent little brutes. Indeed, the water lily itself is a descendent of *Archaefructus sinensis*, the earliest known flowering plant, which was around at least 125 million years ago—considerably before us humans. Frankly, the world does not contain enough herbicide/defoliant to get rid of them all. Nor does it contain enough young girls to pick them, every one.

The ditty from which the line comes is based on a Ukrainian folk song, adapted by Pete Seeger in 1955. The singer also helped to popularize "Kumbaya." He has much to answer for.

Would you like to swing on a star?

An instinctive reaction may be that this sounds like fun, but just stop and think for a minute. The nearest star to Earth is the Sun, which is about 150 million km (100 million miles) away; if you don't count the Sun (perhaps because you've always thought of it as the Sun and not realized that it was a star), the nearest is Proxima Centauri, well over four light years away. Four light years add up to roughly 37,842,800,000,000,000 km (23,513,600,000,000,000 miles) and, at the time of writing, there is no way of getting to Proxima Centauri by public transport. It would cost a fortune in petrol—and be incredibly ungreen—if you took your own car. Even if you get a respectable 20 km per liter (56 miles to the gallon) on the open road, it's about $1,175,680,000,000,000 for a one-way trip. Face it, it just isn't going to happen in the foreseeable future.

Where have you been all my life?

How long have you got? How much detail are you after? And indeed how old are you, compared to me, so at what point in my life would you like me to start?

Statistically speaking, of the approximately 7 billion people on our planet, over half live in just seven countries— China, India, the US, Indonesia, Brazil, Pakistan, and Bangladesh. So the chances are that the "you" whom you were addressing was in one of those. Which may not answer your question with pinpoint accuracy, but what were you expecting?

How do you solve a problem like Maria?

According to the song in *The Sound of Music*, the problems with Maria were manifold. To name just a few, she was prone to climbing trees and scraping her knees, wore curlers beneath her wimple, was always late for chapel, and was a "flibbertijibbet," "will-o'-the-wisp," and "clown." All of which is to say, she was temperamentally unsuited to life as a nun. One solution would have been a much improved careers education while she was at school.

However, such advice clearly having been unavailable to Maria, what could her convent do once they had taken her on? Deciding she was an unsatisfactory novice, they sent her yodeling off to be governess to the children of a rich man, where she was promptly sidetracked from any further thoughts of the religious life and put a spoke in the wheel of Nazism while she was about it. A good result all round. Nowadays, the answer to this, as to so many questions in life, is to hold a TV talent contest, with the winner receiving a starring role in a West End musical.

Where *does* the time go?

Let's assume for the sake of argument that you are not a particle physicist and that your brain reels at the mention of antimatter, quanta, and quarks. In that case, time goes forward, with the result that something that has just happened goes into the past. But if what you are really asking is "Why does time go by so quickly? How can it possibly be nearly Christmas *again*?" it suggests that you are doing interesting things with your life. Scientists at the University of Alberta in Canada conducted research that proved—to their satisfaction at least—that our view of how much time has passed is closely connected to how engrossed we have been in whatever we have been doing. Frankly I don't think this is rocket science, but then we established at the start of this entry that you aren't a rocket scientist . . .

How long has this been going on?

A multiple-choice answer to allow for different interpretations of "this":

a If "this" = the Universe, approximately 13.7 billion years

b If "this" = planet Earth, approximately 4.5 billion years

c If "this" = the earliest form of life on Earth, approximately 3.8 billion years

d If "this" = human life on Earth, approximately 2.5 million years

e If "this" = the human race as we know it (*Homo sapiens sapiens*), about 195,000 years

f If "this" = something more personal, then that is absolutely none of your business, especially if you happen to be an official from the government. But I'll let you in on a secret: it is less than 195,000 years.

How long is a piece of string?

According to popular-science writers Rob Eastaway and Jeremy Wyndham, who have produced a book with this title, it can be infinitely long. This is because of something called fractals: "patterns that continue to reveal similar patterns on a smaller and smaller scale as you zoom in," like a head of broccoli, which can be "dissected" into ever smaller heads of broccoli, all similar in appearance and perfectly formed. This is what happens with a piece of string that is anything other than absolutely straight. It has little kinks in it that, if you care to examine them under a magnifying glass, will be revealed as having more little kinks and more and more until you have to stop counting or your brain will implode.

Do one-legged ducks swim in circles?

Probably not, actually. A duck with one leg would simply use its weight to compensate for any loss of balance, and might well employ its good leg as a sort of fin, allowing it to swim perfectly happily in straight lines. But have you ever seen a one-legged duck? No, I thought not.

Do you know the way to San José?

Certainly, if you are talking about San José, California: it's about 60 km (40 miles) south of San Francisco. It has an airport, so if you happen to be in LA, parking cars and pumping gas, you can fly direct in an hour and ten minutes. There are lots of other places called San José scattered across the world, mostly in Spanish-speaking countries. One is the capital of Costa Rica (there are a few direct flights from LA, but mostly you have to change in Mexico City or San Salvador); others are to be found in Argentina, Bolivia, Brazil, Colombia, Guatemala, Mexico, the Philippines, and Uruguay. Alternatively, there is a San José river in New Mexico, which runs into the Rio Grande. If you head east from the point where the two rivers meet, you will soon find yourself in Amarillo, which will save you having to ask another question that might have been at the back of your mind.

Is it true what they say about Dixie?

Yes, because believe it or not one of the things they say about Dixie is that people keep eating possum until they can't eat any more. Assuming you don't fancy them raw, there are recipes all over the Internet, including instructions on feeding them on milk for ten days before killing them, then hanging them for only a couple of days so that they aren't too gamey. One post claims that "a neighbor of mine used to use raccoon in his Mexican food. They loved raccoon burritos. Possum makes a great meat pie, as does squirrel." Another refers to Southern restaurants using possums and armadillo in their chilli. Vegetarians and the squeamish may choose to stay north of the Mason-Dixon Line.

All the lonely people, where do they all come from?

Lonely people can come from all over the place: there are lots of clichés about being lonely in a crowd or when you are a long-distance runner. The French poet Paul Valéry blamed it on God, who "created man and, finding him not sufficiently alone, gave him a companion to make him feel his solitude more keenly." This is rather maligning God, who, according to the Book of Genesis, was acting with the best intentions: He thought that Adam, the first man, needed a "help meet," so He created Eve. She's the one who promptly got them chucked out of the Garden of Eden, you may remember, so it may be that even God has the odd bad idea.

Despite the fact that the population of the world has more than quadrupled since 1900, there seem to be more lonely people today than ever. A 2006 study by the University of Arizona and Duke University reported that almost 25 percent of respondents lacked even one friend with whom to discuss matters important to them, an increase of over 200 percent on 1985. So perhaps today's lonely people come from those places where more and more of us rush around with headphones in our ears or our heads stuck in laptops, enjoying the fruits of a virtual world at the expense of the real one around us. If only someone could find a way to hook up all those lonely folk . . .

Why can't a woman be more like a man?

Why would she want to, you might well ask? For a start, women can expect to live longer than men in virtually every country in the world. They are also less likely to be the victims of crime, and men are far more prone to suicide. Nor is it possible for a man to achieve the same kind of orgasmic glow that a woman can experience simply by trying on a pair of preposterously expensive shoes.

But assuming she does want to be more like a man, there are several good scientific reasons why she can't. Apart from the obvious physical differences, there are plenty of unseen ones too. For instance, while men are flooded with the aggression-inspiring hormone testosterone, women are rather more effected by estrogen. There are also differences in brain structure (in terms of both size and areas of activity) that ensure men and women process and respond to information in different ways. Add to these physical factors the impact of ancient sociological trends that, until very recently, gave women the role of mothers and home-builders while men were expected to go out and provide. It is no surprise that the different genders can sometimes seem like entirely separate species.

So to summarize: "Because both her body and her brain are constructed differently from a man's" or, if you catch her on a bad day, "Because she just can't, OK?"

Who's on first base?

If you know the Abbott and Costello original, you'll be aware that this isn't a question at all, it is a statement. If you don't, you'll be baffled. Life's a bitch.

(And for the record, the man who was most likely to meet on first base was Pete Rose, the legendary Cincinnati Red who hit a record 3,215 singles in his illustrious career.)

Does my bum look big in this?

Women are notoriously sensitive about the size of their posteriors, sometimes but by no means always with justification. For men there is only one safe answer to this question: no, of course not, dear.

However, this does not mean that women should not

reconsider their phobia of "junk in the trunk," for there is ample evidence that a big behind has a lot to be said for it. Evolutionists consider that a large bottom and wide hips are Nature's indicators of rich fertility, which is always a turn-on at a primitive level. And what of all the great cultural celebrations, from Rubens's callipygean beauties to the "fat-bottomed girls" who "make the rockin' world go round" as celebrated by Queen? According to the World Health Organization, the fattest-bottomed girls are likely to be found in Tonga, where, in 2009, 74.9 percent of females over fifteen were obese. The more robust lady should perhaps consider the words of the eloquent Sir Mix-a-Lot, who joyously admitted in 1992: "I like big butts and I cannot lie." Just ask J-Lo if it's done her any harm. Anyone still unconvinced and oversensitive about the size of her backside could press for the reintroduction of the bustle.

Do bears shit in the woods?

It depends on the bear; the habitat of one of the best-known species does not usually include forested or woodland areas. Although polar bears may make their dens on land, and under certain conditions will move into relatively ice-free areas where there may be a few trees, generally they have no option but to defecate on ice or snow, in water, or on barren tundra, since there are no woods in their, er, neck of the woods . . .

Why a duck?

To make sense of this question you have to include the supplementary query, "Why-a-no-chicken?" The differences between the two birds are considerable: one is a waterfowl with webbed feet, a flat bill designed for feeding on aquatic vegetation, and a readily identifiable quacking call; the other lives on land, pecks at seeds on the ground, and in most breeds the male boasts a prominent comb and piercing cry. There should in theory be no confusion. However, in practice, the question comes from a Marx Brothers film (*The Cocoanuts*, 1929), so confusion is the object of the exercise and making sense of the question is simply not going to happen.

CHAPTER THREE

Who wants to be a millionaire?

Questions of finance and business

Is there anyone who hasn't sometimes felt the truth of the maxim that, although money doesn't buy happiness, it allows you to be miserable in comfort?

Who wants to be a millionaire?

An enormous number of people, apparently. The TV quiz show of this name has been running for over twenty years, has aired in more than a hundred countries, and has made people from everywhere, from Chile to Germany, millionaires in their local currency. However, once upon a time, people of a certain age wowed by Cole Porter's score for *High Society* would burst into song and warble, "I don't!" in answer to this question. But, as they would also have had you believe that they were unimpressed by country estates, supersonic planes, or wallowing in champagne, they were clearly a dying breed.

Am I made of money?

Almost certainly not. Indeed, if you have seen the James Bond film *Goldfinger* you may well believe that being made of money (in the sense of being painted with gold, at least) is fatal. That's because covering every inch of the body in a substance like gold prevents the skin from breathing, thereby causing death. In fact, gold is one of the most nonreactive substances around, which is why you can have fillings made of it and claim (if it really matters that much to you) that part of you is indeed made of money.

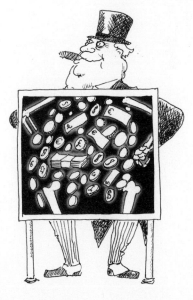

Has your mother sold her mangle?

She may well have done: the invention of the automatic washing machine in the first decade of the twentieth century spun a lot of the excess water out of laundry and made the mangle (or the wringer, if you are reading this in American) largely obsolete, although some still extol its virtues as an alternative to ironing. Should this appeal to you, or should you fancy an antique version for use as a "feature" in a garden or farmhouse-style kitchen, they are readily available on eBay.

How much is that doggie in the window?

Never mind the price. Do not even think about buying a dog that you see in a shop window, unless it is made of porcelain and meant to sit on the fireplace. If you want a live one, go to a recognized breeder or a rescue center. The going rate at time of writing is £95 from Battersea Dog's Home in London and between $75 and $175 from the US Animal League. What's more, you'll be giving money to a good cause, rather than to the sort of charlatan who keeps doggies in confined spaces in shop windows. On a less dictatorial note, however, once you are there, there is no harm in choosing (or allowing yourself to be chosen by) the one with the waggly tail.

Who will buy this wonderful morning?

Nobody, presumably, mornings not normally being for sale. But it would be a hard-hearted person who said that to Oliver in the film named after him. He's been arrested for pickpocketing (unsurprisingly—nobody who looks that sweet and innocent can possibly be cut out for a life of crime), rescued by the kindly Mr. Brownlow, and is about to be recaptured by evil Bill Sikes and dragged back to Fagin's den. He really doesn't need to be disillusioned about the purchasability of beautiful mornings. But the sad truth is that if he wants to hang on to this one, he'd be better off asking the Artful Dodger to nick it for him.

CHAPTER FOUR

Is the Pope a Catholic?

Questions about the meaning of life

Who is as the wise man? And who knowest the interpretation of a thing? If even the Bible can't answer questions such as these, what hope is there for the rest of us? Wouldn't we all be happier if we had a firmer grasp on the philosophical concepts that might help to explain life, death, and the hereafter (if applicable)?

Is the Pope a Catholic?

Yes. Actually, he's the leader of the entire Roman Catholic Church, as well as being Bishop of Rome and head of the independent sovereign state of the Vatican City. However, the first Pope, so many Catholics believe, was Saint Peter, who was born a Jew. Old-fashioned or conservative Anglicans would insist on asking, "Is the Pope a *Roman* Catholic?" partly because of the Great Schism in the church in the eleventh century that led to the formation of the Roman Catholic, Western Orthodox, and Eastern Orthodox Churches, and partly because the Nicene Creed as used in the Anglican liturgy refers to "one holy catholic and apostolic church." In this context the word means "universal, all-embracing," which makes asking whether the Pope is a Catholic meaningless. But as the question is usually posed in a shoulder-shrugging, what-can-you-do-about-it sort of way, it probably doesn't matter much. It is often bracketed with the less tasteful question about the defecatory habits of bears (see page 41).

For what shall it profit a man, if he shall gain the whole world but lose his own soul?

Not a lot, is Jesus's message, as He encourages His disciples to make sacrifices in order to follow Him and, in due course, make it into the Kingdom of Heaven. It's an example of the benefits of taking the long-term view. If you are tempted to disagree, be warned by the example of Richard Rich in Robert Bolt's play *A Man for All Seasons*: he gives false evidence against the saintly Thomas More and as a reward is made Attorney-General for Wales. Thomas, under sentence of death, says mournfully, "Why, Richard, it profits a man nothing to give his soul for the whole world . . . but for Wales?" Quite.

O death, where is thy sting?
O grave, where is thy victory?

Lost and gone for ever, if you believe Saint Paul. His point is that at the moment of "the last trump," the trumpet shall sound and "the dead shall be raised incorruptible." In other words, thanks to the efforts of God and Christ, mortal man will win out over Death, who will be "swallowed up in victory" and will have to go and find someone else to torment. All of which will happen "in the twinkling of an eye," so there will be no opportunity for Death to lodge an appeal or even to whine that it's not fair.

Which of you by taking thought can add one cubit unto his stature?

No one, of course. Thinking isn't the way to get taller, particularly not a cubit taller. A cubit is a measure based on the length of the forearm, from the elbow to the tip of the middle finger, perhaps 46 cm (18 in) in an average-sized man. So although you may *feel* a bit taller after a yoga class, in reality growing as much as an inch (2.5 cm, the width of a man's thumb) would be extraordinary and growing a cubit eighteen times more so. If you really want to be taller, you could save a lot of trouble by investing in a pair of stiletto heels.

Can the leopard change his spots?

The prophet Jeremiah's natural history may have been slightly at fault when he posed this question. The answer all depends on how long you give the leopard to achieve its transformation. You certainly won't witness it with your own eyes but, in accordance with Darwinist theory, some subspecies did indeed change their spots over several generations through natural selection so as to be better adapted to their environments. One such was *Panthera pardus adersi* (or the Zanzibar leopard), now almost certainly extinct. When Zanzibar became separated from the African mainland at the end of the last ice age, the animal gradually became smaller than its mainland cousins and its spots, or "rosettes," reduced in size accordingly. We can also point to the panther, which is an all-black—or "melanistic"—leopard or jaguar, whose dark "rosettes" have, through genetic mutation, become virtually indiscernible against its equally dark background fur. None of which information Jeremiah would have had to hand.

Que sais-je?

Or, in other words: "What do I know?" Some might answer: *"Rien. On ne peut être sûr de rien."* (Before translating it for the non-Francophones as: "Nothing. One can be certain of nothing.")

While that may sound a little pessimistic, it is a position adopted by countless great philosophers throughout history. It was the motto of the sixteenth-century French philosopher Montaigne, and fifty years later his fellow-countryman Descartes made the famous assertion: *"Cogito ergo sum"* or "I think, therefore I am." Essentially, Descartes was saying that to have thoughts is to prove you exist, but that is the only fact you can be truly sure of (as there may be a demon trying to deceive you on everything else). The rock group U2 added their take on things when they bombarded adoring crowds with the message "Everything You Know Is Wrong" on their epic *Zooropa* world tour of the 1990s. Though that may simply have been a sneaky tactic to sow seeds of doubt in the minds of any fans who'd formed an opinion on the price of the merchandise they were being encouraged to buy.

Hath not a Jew eyes?

Yes, of course. And if you want to persist and ask "Hath not a Jew hands, organs, dimensions, senses, affections, passions? fed with the same food, hurt with the same weapons, subject to the same diseases, healed by the same means, warmed and cooled by the same winter and summer, as a Christian is? If you prick us, do we not bleed? If you tickle us, do we not laugh? If you poison us, do we not die? And if you wrong us, shall we not revenge?" the answers are yes every time, until you come to the last question. Then the answer, if you happen to be a Jew in Shakespearian Venice, is "Well, you can try, pal, but I don't give much for your chances."

What judgment shall I dread, doing no wrong?

The judgment of a Christian court, unfortunately, if you still happen to be a Jew in Shakespearian Venice (see previous entry). They'll confiscate all your worldly goods and make you become a Christian to boot. Amazingly, nobody seems to have thought this was at all reprehensible in Shakespeare's day.

Today, the Universal Declaration of Human Rights (Article 11) enshrines the right of everybody to be presumed innocent of a penal offence "until proved guilty according to law in a public trial at which they have had all the guarantees necessary for their defense." In the vast majority of countries, this means that the burden of proof rests with the prosecution; that is to say, they must prove the accused's guilt, rather than the accused having to prove their innocence. That is not to say that there aren't some apparent anomalies. For instance, in libel cases it often falls to the defendant to prove that what they published was accurate and fair, rather than for the prosecution to prove that it was untrue.

Who can control his fate?

Who indeed? Certainly not anyone who—to take the case of Othello—gets it into his head that his wife has been unfaithful, refuses to listen to her protestations of innocence, and murders her in a fit of jealous rage. Guys, let's take a moment to point up a moral here: sometimes, just sometimes, when a woman asks you to listen to what she is saying, it may be worth paying attention.

Of course, your view of how much control of your fate you have depends on whether you believe in free will, a question that has vexed the greatest minds of both the Eastern and Western philosophical traditions. Are our lives predestined from the outset by a god or some other higher force so that we never have real free will, even when we think we do? Are our decisions preprogrammed by our biological makeups or social backgrounds? Does what has happened historically determine what will happen in the future? Or do we indeed have free will after all?

Frankly, if such eminent thinkers as Epicurus, Saint Paul, Thomas Hobbes, Schopenhauer, David Hume, John

Locke, Jean-Paul Sartre, and Thomas Nagel (to name the merest few) have failed to come up with an irrefutable answer, I don't think I'm going to manage it either.

What! Can the Devil speak true?

The thing about the Devil is he has to speak *plausibly*. Truth doesn't really come into it—or rather, it comes into it only if telling the truth is going to serve the Devil's purposes. Take the example of Shakespeare's *Macbeth*, in which these words were first spoken. The three witches— let's agree that they are the Devil's agents or this whole discussion becomes pointless—have prophesied that Macbeth will be "king hereafter." Once this improbable idea has been planted, Macbeth is going to commit whatever evil deeds it takes to make it come true, and of course there is nothing to beat an evil deed when it comes to serving the Devil's purposes. As a first step, what Macbeth does is talk to his wife, which turns out to be a very bad idea indeed.

To be or not to be . . . ?

Well, of course, that is the question, at least for Hamlet. Is it nobler to put up with the crap that life slings at us or to decide that enough is enough? The World Health Organization estimates that globally a million people per year plump for the latter and take their own lives (that's about 16 people per 100,000). Hamlet goes on to say that the prospect of falling asleep and never waking up to have to deal with life's turmoil is attractive, but the dreams we may have in that sleep of death are a worry, or indeed "the rub." Unfortunately, this isn't going to be resolved until someone comes back from the dead and disseminates some reliable inside information. If that bothers you, don't book Dignitas any time soon . . .

Dreams? No, it's not so bad really.

Whence are we, and why are we? Of what scene/the actors and spectators?

This is one of those foolish metaphysical questions that become simpler if they are broken down into component parts. The first two are straightforward: most of us come from our mother's womb, as the result of an act of fruitful sex between our parents (oh, stop squirming, you know it's true). The third is more difficult, because at any given point we are all at such different phases in our lives: taking part in our own christening, wedding or driving test, or mere lookers-on at a football match or in the cinema.

According to a 2009 US Bureau of Labor Statistics survey, a fair amount of the average American's time goes on "leisure," most of it rather more passive than active. The employed American works on average 7.5 hours per day during the working week, with a further two hours spent on household chores. A princely five hours plus goes on leisure time, which can encompass anything from running a marathon to socializing to sitting in front of the goggle box (the latter, rather sadly, being the most popular pastime by some distance, coming in at an average 2.5–3 hours a day). Tellingly, the younger generation spends a mere five minutes a day at the weekend reading, while averaging an hour on the computer. So altogether there seems to be rather more "spectating" than "acting."

Having said that, the poet Shelley, who wrote these lines, would have us believe that it doesn't matter, because in the end we will all meet "massed in death." Even those who are remembered by those who live on after them will be forgotten when those people die too, if you follow his reasoning. "What's the point?" might have been a briefer and more pertinent question.

How often have I said to you that when you have eliminated the impossible, whatever remains, however improbable, must be the truth?

Actually, only once on record (in *The Sign of Four*, 1890), but doubtless many other times: this is Sherlock Holmes and he did like his maxims. He probably said, "You know my methods; apply them" at every opportunity, too.

What is to be done?

If in doubt, have a revolution. According to Vladimir Ilyich Lenin this was the answer to any question of social or political importance, and it worked for him—in the short term, at least. However, that does rather overlook the 15 million people who became casualties in the four-year civil war that followed. In lieu of revolution, a nice cup of tea and a slice of cake can cure most ills, while others swear that a bit of retail therapy can solve even the thorniest of problems.

What does a woman want?

Sigmund Freud claimed to have spent thirty years researching into the feminine soul without finding an answer to this question. Twenty-first-century cinemagoers could have saved him a lot of anguish: in the film *What Women Want* it took Mel Gibson only a couple of hours of screen time to discover that, never mind all Sigmund's obsessing about sex organs, a man being just a teensy bit less obnoxious was always acceptable to women. Asked in an interview what *he* thought women wanted, Mel revealed that he had given the matter almost as much thought as Sigmund had: "After about twenty years of marriage, I'm finally starting to scratch the surface of that one. And I think the answer lies somewhere between conversation and chocolate." Most women would agree that he was getting warm.

Further evidence came in a survey of 2010 by a British pawnbrokers, Borro.com, no less. At the top of the list of what a woman wanted was a wonderful relationship with her mother. Heartening indeed. Good friends also featured very highly. But a loving boyfriend came in only fifth, a little below mobile phones.

Where do I begin?

Try page 1.

If, on examining himself, a man finds nothing to reproach himself for, what worries and fears can he have?

Lots of things, surely? The website psychology.about.com claims that phobias (from the Greek *phobos* meaning fear) are the most common mental disorder in the US and lists no fewer than ninety-four of them, ranging from the sensible (pyrophobia, fear of fire) through the slightly weird (porphyrophobia, fear of the color purple) to the downright inconvenient (podophobia, fear of feet, or koinoniphobia, fear of rooms). And these are full-blown phobias: what about all the little niggles such as forgetting an anniversary or drinking from the wrong glass at a formal dinner? In fact, it is all so worrying that, if you'll excuse me, I'm just going to have to go and lie down for a minute.

What's the use of worrying?

None, according to the World War I song—it never was worthwhile. This sunny attitude cropped up again and again in the course of the twentieth century, when various other songwriters advised looking for the silver lining, accentuating the positive, and always looking on the bright side of life. As it happens, modern medicine is with them all the way: it recognizes that excessive worry causes all sorts of unpleasant symptoms from lack of concentration to bowel problems. If you find that worrying, try not to think about it: you'll only make yourself ill.

A quoi bon?

This may look like the French for "*Cui bono?*" (see page 18), but in fact it is more like "What's the use?" or "What's the point?" Very often, if we seek to identify the true motivations for our actions we will find them far from edifying. All too commonly, "the point" is greed, ambition, jealousy, revenge, or the realization of personal desires. However, Shelley E. Taylor, a psychologist at UCLA, has put forward a less cynical view. In *The Tending Instinct: How Nurturing Is Essential to Who We Are and How We Live*, she has argued that we are equally hardwired to act by our desire to nurture others and look after their needs.

Nonetheless, for many the natural answer to our question "*A quoi bon?*" is "Not much point, really, now you come to mention it." This is particularly true if the question is extended, as it often is, to "*A quoi bon l'amour?*" The poet Shelley could have learned something from the succinctness of this approach, I feel (see *Whence are we, and why are we? Of what scene/the actors and spectators?* on page 61).

What's it all about, Alfie?

Anyone who has seen the classic 1966 film *Alfie* (directed by Lewis Gilbert and written by Bill Naughton) knows that it's about love. Or it is in the end. Not in the beginning, though. In the beginning, as far as Alfie is concerned, it is all about getting women into bed. The song that asks the question suggests that there is more to life than that, and Alfie comes gradually to realize that this is true. By the end of the film, he's got some money in his pocket, decent clothes, and a fancy car—but he ain't got peace of mind. And without that, he asks himself, "Wot's it all about?" Which is where we came in.

Who do you think you are?

This is a question traditionally posed to some big-'ead with a high opinion of himself. In 1991, two academics, N. W. Van Yperen and A. P. Buunk, gave the condition of Toobigforyourbootsitis (in which you overestimate your personal qualities and underestimate your weaknesses) a grand new name: "illusory superiority." This is often to be witnessed on TV talent shows when people of notably little talent perform in the belief that they are, in fact, unrecognized genii.

In 2008 Professor Adrian Furnham of University College London revealed the results of a study indicating that the male of the species is rather more prone than the female to illusory superiority. Having evaluated the results of twenty-five studies of IQ results by gender, Professor Furnham was able to conclude that, while both genders have the same average IQ, men typically overestimate their score by five points while women underestimate by the same factor.

In recent times, the question "Who do you think you are?" has been asked by television program makers keen on unearthing the family histories of celebrities. But in case the celebrities assume that they must thus be someone pretty darned interesting, they should consider the cautionary tale of TV presenter Michael Parkinson, a man you would have thought had led a more than averagely interesting life. Approached to feature in the series, he warned the BBC researchers that he had failed to uncover anything noteworthy in his own ancestry; six weeks of hard graft later they had to admit that he was right and abandon the idea of making a program about him. Who's to say that that isn't likely to be true of most of us?

Whose life is it, anyway?

Yours, pal. Or is it? In the play of this name by Brian Clark (later made into a film starring Richard Dreyfuss), a sculptor is paralyzed after an accident. Creative, articulate, and deeply frustrated, he sees no purpose in life as a quadriplegic and wants to be left to die; his doctor is determined to save him. To be or not to be, that is the question, you might think, if you happen to have read page 60.

Am I right or am I right?

An instinctive response may be, "No, you damn well aren't," uttered with or without raised hackles. If you're feeling less aggressive, "*Que sais-je?*" (see page 55) or "Who do you think you are?" (see page 70) are possible alternatives.

Sadly, though, there will always be cocksure individuals convinced of their own rightness in all walks of life. Consider the case of former President Richard Nixon. Having brought shame upon the highest office in the world, he delivered a resignation speech that managed to include an admission that his judgments were wrong while maintaining the sense that he had been absolutely in the right all along. Witness:

"I regret deeply any injuries that may have been done in the course of the events that led to this decision. I would say only that if some of my judgments were wrong, and some were wrong, they were made in what I believed at the time to be the best interest of the Nation."

Another man famed for his confidence in his own actions was the beloved manager of Nottingham Forest Football Club, Brian Clough. When asked how he dealt with players who questioned his judgement, he replied:

"We talk about it for twenty minutes and then we decide I was right."

Is that a fact?

Words usually uttered by an interlocutor trying to take you down a peg or two. In general, ignore them. But always keep in mind that, however much you think you're right about something, there is always the chance you're wrong.

Think what a fool you would feel if you insisted—as most of us would—that the Great Wall of China was the only man-made structure visible from space, only to discover, when you had finished laying down the law, that it simply wasn't true. (There is, in fact, no point in space from which the Great Wall is the only visible man-made structure.) Or if you had been a member of the medieval Roman Catholic Church that excommunicated Galileo and banned his *Dialogue* until 1822 for its heretical claim that the Earth was not at the center of the Universe. It's worth being aware that a "fact" can depend on who believes it and at what moment in time—who knows what the future will tell us about the running battle between the believers and sceptics of global warming?

Do they know it's Christmas?

They probably know, but do they care? The song of this title, written by Bob Geldof and Midge Ure in 1984, was recorded by a host of stars under the Band Aid banner, in aid of the victims of the famine then devastating Ethiopia. It sold a million copies in the United States alone and raised millions of dollars in the process, but that doesn't reduce the pertinence of the question: is a country with a long history of famine, civil war, and rigged elections likely to have much energy to spare for mistletoe, drunken office parties, and gross consumerism?

CHAPTER FIVE

Et tu, Brute?

Questions from literature, history, and politics

Where would we be without Shakespeare, who posed some of the most unanswerable questions in literature? And if ever that became too serious, what would we do without politicians to lampoon?

Et tu, Brute?

Anyone who asks you this is quoting Shakespeare's version of the assassination of Julius Caesar in 44 BC. Caesar was dead before he could hear Brutus's reply, but it can only have been "Yes, I'm afraid so." If you are being asked this question you have presumably committed some act of gross treachery, so "Yes, I'm afraid so" is your best answer too. If you are feeling penitent, that is.

Here was a Caesar! When comes such another?

About a year after the assassination mentioned in the previous entry. This is when Caesar's great-nephew and adopted heir, Octavian, became coruler of Rome as a member of the Second Triumvirate. Eventually he acquired sole rule, and declared himself Emperor, possibly failing to note the anomaly of a republic headed by an emperor. In 26 BC the Senate voted him the title "Augustus," the name by which he is best known to posterity. "Caesar" quickly developed its modern imperial meaning: it was used as a title by many succeeding Roman emperors and later adopted into other languages, such as the German Kaiser and the Russian Czar or Tsar. But if Mark Antony had actually asked the question (as opposed to Shakespeare making it up) it would have been an anachronism: at the time "Caesar" was nothing more impressive than Julius's surname.

What did your last slave die of?

The suggestion is that the slave died of overwork, or perhaps of boredom through being asked to perform tedious tasks such as shutting the door, passing the TV remote, or making a cup of tea—all to stop the person making the requests having to get off his backside and do the jobs himself. Or herself. There's nothing gender-specific intended here. Sadly, people who are self-centred enough to make others run around after them tend to be immune to sarcasm, so asking this question could be a waste of breath.

One should spare greater thought for the millions of real slaves transported from Africa to the New World. It is estimated that somewhere around 11 million made the arduous journey between the fifteenth and nineteenth centuries, of whom 10–20 percent died en route (to say nothing of the countless more who lost their lives after arrival). Leading causes of death included dysentery, smallpox, and suicide. It puts the modern use of the question into perspective, doesn't it?

Is this a dagger which I see before me?

No, it's a book. Or, if you're Macbeth, it may be a figment of the imagination. If you're in the sort of state where you are imagining daggers, you are probably in the sort of state where you can go off and commit murder, so it might be a good idea to sit quietly and finish reading this book in the hope that the mood will pass.

Would you buy a used car from this man?

In 1968 the Democrats produced a campaign poster with a photograph of Richard Nixon and this question as the caption. They thought not, and this was before the Watergate scandal made his name a byword for trickiness. However, a woman called Liz Murphy bought Barack Obama's used Jeep Cherokee and later sold it for more than twice the sum she paid for it. So, I guess it depends who is president.

Who is Silvia?

She's the daughter of the Duke of Milan in Shakespeare's *Two Gentlemen of Verona*, beloved of Valentine, one of the "two gentlemen." She's also "holy, fair, and wise," should you be interested. The name comes from the Latin for "wood," and the other famous Silvia was the mother of Romulus and Remus, legendary founders of Rome. She allegedly became pregnant by the god Mars, so was clearly no holier, fairer, or wiser than she ought to be. On the other hand, all our swains commended Shakespeare's Silvia, so if it's a swain you're after, you could do worse than adopt the name.

Romeo, Romeo, wherefore art thou Romeo?

The answer to this is not, as is often supposed, "I'm down in the garden, staring up at your balcony and freezing half to death" but "Because that's what my parents decided to call me when I was born"—*wherefore* meaning not *where* but *why*. In fact it's a silly question, because it isn't Romeo's given name that anyone objects to, it's his surname. Romeo and Juliet's families, the Montagues and the Capulets, are at loggerheads and the youngsters' romance is never going to find favor with their parents. So when Juliet soliloquizes that Romeo should doff his name and take her instead, she should really be asking him to doff the Montague part of it—which would have scanned every bit as well.

The same speech includes the subsidiary question "What's in a name?" which Juliet answers herself with the not obviously relevant "A rose by any other name would smell as sweet." She seems to be ignoring the fact that Romeo is not a rose and that his personal hygiene is not the issue here.

The name's Stan actually, miss.

What is the use of a book without pictures or conversation?

So wondered Alice. Once upon a time such a book would have been intended simply to be read: to impart information, enjoyment, or insight into the human condition. Nowadays, with some 14 percent of adults in the US and fractionally more in the UK being functionally illiterate, it could be argued that pictures at least are useful in helping those for whom reading is a struggle to work out what the book is about. Which may be why we have put some illustrations in this one.

What price glory?

Quite a high price, some would say. The question was posed in the title of a play about World War I. Something upward of 16 million people (9,750,000 military, 6,800,000 civilian) were killed and 21 million wounded in the war itself, not to mention the 50 million plus who died in the Spanish flu epidemic that followed. I'd call that high.

Who's afraid of Virginia Woolf?

Anybody who has to study *To the Lighthouse* can be forgiven a certain amount of trepidation: Woolf is not the easiest of authors if you don't spend your waking hours pondering the transience of life, art, and philosophy.

However, one man definitely not afraid of Virginia was Roy Campbell, a South African–born poet much admired by the likes of T. S. Eliot. Campbell moved with his wife, Mary, to Sissinghurst in Kent in the late 1920s, where he met Vita Sackville-West and was introduced to the Bloomsbury Set (including Woolf). No doubt a little narked that Mary and Vita promptly embarked on an affair (which also prompted a fit of jealousy from Virginia, who craved Vita's attention), Campbell undertook a campaign against that louche Bloomsbury lot. It culminated in 1931 with the publication of *The Georgiad*, complete with impassioned attacks against both Vita and Virginia.

How do they know?

This is said to have been asked by the poet and wit
Dorothy Parker on hearing of the death of President
Calvin Coolidge. Calvin was famously a man of few words,
but it is unlikely that on a physiological level he showed
fewer vital signs than the rest of us. When he died—of
a heart attack, in 1933, at the age of sixty—his medical
attendants presumably noted that his heart had ceased
to function, always something of a dead giveaway where
dying's concerned (not breathing's another). The fact
that he ceased to file copy for his syndicated newspaper
column might also sooner or later have alerted his editors
and readers to the fact that something was wrong.

LBJ, LBJ, how many kids have you killed today?

"Too damned many" is a good ballpark figure. For the benefit of the young and unhistorically minded, LBJ was Lyndon Baines Johnson, President of the United States from November 1963 until January 1969, a period that covered the height of the war in Vietnam. According to the US National Archives, which gives annual figures for American deaths in the conflict from 1965 onward (when the rate increased significantly), in the period 1965–68 the toll was 35,751. As a very crude average, that works out at about 24 lives per day. Not all of the Vietnam casualties were LBJ's fault. But a lot of them were.

CHAPTER SIX

Shall I compare thee to a summer's day?

Questions of social intercourse

Is there anything more pleasant than a friendly greeting or a solicitous enquiry after one's health? Or anything more irritating than the lack of concern for others that is the basis of ill manners?

How do you do?

According to the etiquette books, this is not a question at all; it is a courteous but otherwise meaningless form of words used on greeting another person. The only correct answer to it is "How do *you* do?" Posh people consider "Pleased to meet you" and any response along the lines of "Quite well, thank you" boring—or common, if you prefer. Nowadays, on the other hand, people increasingly regard it as a question about their health, and proceed to answer it. In detail.

"How are you?" is similarly not a question. Unless the person asking knows that you have been ill or having a difficult time, they really want you to say, "I'm fine, thanks, how are you?" which allows them to carry on talking about something more interesting, such as themselves. Hence the immortal line, overheard at a cocktail party: "But that's enough about me, let's talk about you. What do *you* think of me?"

Where do you go to, my lovely?

So the singer Peter Sarstedt demanded in 1969 of a certain Marie-Claire. "Mind your own business," she may have responded, especially when he qualified his question with the words "when you're alone in your bed." But as she spent her days gadding about with the jet set, worrying about the evenness of her suntan and sipping brandy without getting her lips wet, she was probably only too pleased to have a bit of peace and quiet once she got home.

For what do we live, but to make sport for our neighbors, and laugh at them in our turn?

So says Mr. Bennet to his daughter Elizabeth in *Pride and Prejudice*. On the face of it, the question is stupid: we live for a good deal more. (At its most biological level, we exist to propagate the species, an activity that tends to be more enjoyable than sitting around in a stuffy drawing room, making polite conversation with a bunch of local bores over a cup of insipid tea.) Reality TV has rather changed all that, however: not only have people apparently lost any capacity for embarrassment, but they seem nowadays actively to seek humiliation. Jane Austen's characters married (an obsession with them) for wealth, position, and, if they were lucky, happiness. Couples today do so in order to appear on *Wife Swap*. At least if you were living in a Jane Austen novel you could hope for a happy ending. Then again, the American poet Ralph Waldo Emerson said of Austen that "Her characters live in such a wretchedly narrow view of life, that suicide would be more respectable."

Are you going to Scarborough Fair?

Unlikely, as it hasn't existed since 1788, but it was a big thing in its day. It ran from the Feast of the Assumption of the Virgin Mary (August 15) to Michaelmas Day (September 29)—that's quite a party. Anyone who hates the Simon and Garfunkel version of the song of that title as much as any right-thinking person must should try listening to Bob Dylan and Johnny Cash duetting on "Girl from the North Country," a variant of the song.

You talkin' to me?

It depends on how many other people are in the room. The fewer other options there are, the more likely it is that the person in question is talking to you. Unless he or she has a squint, of course, in which case the waiter in the far corner may be the target audience.

Was it something I said?

It may well have been. You can't be too careful. Everything we say is so open to interpretation and misinterpretation. The eighteenth-century satirist Jonathan Swift hit the nail on the head when he wrote, "One of the best rules in conversation is, never to say a thing which any of the company can reasonably wish had been left unsaid." Beware, too, the clangers that can be dropped as a result of tactlessness or embarrassment. As the novelist and poet Ernest Bramah put it, "Although there exist many thousand subjects for elegant conversation, there are persons who cannot meet a cripple without talking about feet." (You can tell that was written a long time ago. Anyone who used the word "cripple" in this sense today would rightly be adjudged as having said "something.")

What's up, Doc?

As with *How you doin'?* (page 140) and *How do you do?* (page 92), many people make the mistake of assuming that this is a genuine question. Unless you are a member of the medical profession, this is unlikely. As used by the cartoon character Bugs Bunny, it doesn't mean much more than "What's going on?" and is a general-purpose, unimpressed taunt directed at his archenemy, the hapless hunter Elmer Fudd. Bugs also routinely makes fun of Elmer's speech impediment, allowing the scriptwriters to give their cartoons titles such as *Wabbit Twouble* and *The Wacky Wabbit*. Oh, how we laughed before political correctness came along and spoilt it all. (Still, at least he didn't say "cwipple" . . .)

Shall I compare thee to a summer's day?

The answer to this depends on your attitude to the person asking the question: it could range from, "That would be charming, thank you" to "Oh, for God's sake, give me a break." But if he/she goes on to say that you are more lovely and more temperate than the average summer's day, less likely to shake the darling buds of May (whatever that means) and less likely than the sun to have your beauty dimmed by clouds passing in front of it, it would be hard not to be flattered (even if you know he's nicked his fancy talk from Shakespeare).

That said, it is worth noting that normal core body temperature is 37°C (98°F), while an average summer's day in Shakespeare's native Stratford-upon-Avon is 16°C (61°F). So if you are prone to take offence, you could read into the words that the speaker is somehow suggesting you're a bit frigid. And beware anyone offering "Shall I compare thee to a wet Sabbath in Scotland?" He or she may not be that into you.

Can you hear me, Major Tom?

Sadly, no. According to the 1969 David Bowie song "Space Oddity," something has gone badly wrong with Major Tom's spaceship and he will not be hearing anything ever again. Particularly as even the loudest unamplified sound (such as a bomb going off) can rarely be heard over a distance of more than 300 km (200 miles) and usually a good deal less. Nowhere near far enough to reach eardrums drifting through space. The fact that Major Tom had really made the grade may have been some consolation—if he had heard it.

Who rattled your cage?

As it would be pointless to ask this of anyone who was not in a cage or who *was* in a cage but unable to speak, it is likely that any reply is going to come from a parrot. But although some African gray parrots are said to have extensive vocabularies, they are better at identifying familiar objects such as keys and bananas than at answering open-ended questions concerning the identity of unknown individuals. So, as with *What did your last slave die of?* (page 80), you may find that asking this question is a waste of breath. The same could be said of . . .

What are you, a man or a mouse?

. . . because the only self-respecting answer to this is a squeak. Unless you're female, of course, in which case the self-respecting answer is a spike heel applied, with great force, to your interlocutor's instep.

Are you blind as well as stupid?

You're unlikely to be blind, as you are reading this. You may or may not be stupid. This question is not to be confused with . . .

Don't you see?

. . . because in this instance "see" means "understand" rather than anything to do with vision. Though, ironically, there are none so blind as those who will not see.

Have you taken leave of your senses?

Another pointless question, because no one who has taken leave of their senses is going to give a reliable answer. However, anyone giving the response "Yes" or even "That's for me to know and you to find out" might be worth questioning further. If, however, the questionee replies "Present my compliments to Marshal Ney, and tell him that I wish the cavalry to advance against Wellington's left," then you will have got your answer. The same applies to . . .

Are you mad?

If you use "mad" in the British sense of "insane," you can't expect a satisfactory response (see previous entry). If you mean it in the American sense of "angry" and the answer is "Yes," you could be in trouble.

Are you color-blind?

Frequently addressed to cyclists who have just ridden through a red light, this assumes the answer, "No, I am perfectly capable of distinguishing between red and green. I merely don't give a toss about the rules of the road. I also know that a cyclist requires no licence that can be endorsed for infringements, and that the police don't give a toss about infringing cyclists."

Have you no sense?/Have you no manners?

If you are being asked either of these questions, you have probably just done something either extremely silly or extremely rude, thereby demonstrating that the answer is "Yes, I do have no manners." But if in the process you have done something to your own advantage, such as grabbing the last piece of cake or riding a bicycle through a red light without being crushed by a 42-ton 8-axle semi, you may feel it is worth putting up with a little sarcasm.

Are you pulling my leg?

Very probably yes. Anybody credulous enough to have to ask this question is almost certainly being teased. That is assuming it is asked in the idiomatic sense. If someone is literally tugging on your lower limb, the effect should be sufficiently obvious to render the question unnecessary.

It has been suggested that the first person who might have asked this was an old Scottish woman known as Aunt Meg. Having been convicted of a crime of which she was innocent because of the trickery of another, she was sentenced to hang. The local preacher is said to have tugged on her legs while she was on the gallows to bring death upon her as quickly and mercifully as possible. Thus, she had her leg pulled after becoming the victim of someone else's deception.

Is it 'cos I is black?

Certainly not, in the case of Ali G, because he wasn't black at all. That was the point. He was pretending to be black in order to seem more interesting than he was. Whether or not he succeeded remains a matter of personal opinion. It is, incidentally, illegal to discriminate against anyone on grounds of race, color, ethnic origin, etc. However, a white coal miner who had gone to the pub without having taken a shower before leaving the pit might well, and justifiably, be discriminated against on the grounds of his skin color.

What's not to like?

Surely a matter for the individual: there are all sorts of things that you might happen not to like, from international terrorism to songs by Hannah Montana if you are over the age of twelve. In fact, a 2009 survey by food company Lactofree attempted to find the one hundred things that most "aren't to like." Topping the list were antisocial youths, streaking ahead of motorists who drive up the back of you, people with bad personal hygiene, individuals who eat with their mouth open, and rude shop staff. And that was but the tip of the iceberg . . .

How cool is that?

A question usually expecting the answer "Very, very cool indeed." Which might be about as cool as, say, driving around with the Fonz in a '57 Caddy, looking up at the stars from a beach in Rio or watching a dog skateboarding. Those who can't get enough of cool should be sure to make time for a visit to Antarctica, where the average annual temperature reached a record low of −89°C (−129°F) in 1983.

Would I lie to you?

As a rule of thumb, a poll by the Science Museum in London discovered that men tell on average 1,092 lies a year (or about three a day) and women 728 (near enough two a day). So my answer is, "Quite possibly, especially if you're a guy."

Don't you know who I am?

This question is rhetorical because it is in fact a statement, to whit: "I am a very famous/important/rich/well-connected etc. personage and I am offended by: your refusal to put up with my lecherous advances/your comments about my drunken, loutish, and insulting behavior/my verbal and/or physical assaults upon your staff/the fact that you have placed me and my party at a rickety table for three by the entrance to the gentleman's lavatory." There are only two possible responses: (a) "No, haven't a clue, chum"; and (b) "Yes, you are Lindsay Lohan/Donald Trump/Paris Hilton. May I have your autograph?" The question is very often followed by the threat "I'll see you never work in this town again."

Anyone arrogant enough to ask the question might like to consider that as many as 2.5 percent of the population have the potential to suffer from a congenital condition called prosopagnosia, or "face-blindness." It is an ailment that leaves the sufferer unable to recognize the features of even those people closest to them, such as a parent or spouse. If you reply to the above question with an,

"I'm dreadfully sorry but I have prosopagnosia," not only are you likely to bamboozle your interrogator (as they rush off to find a medical dictionary) but you will almost certainly make him think twice before posing the same question to somebody else.

CHAPTER SEVEN

Does your mother know you're out?

Questions of domestic life

Why is it that our nearest and dearest, those
with whom we interact every day of our lives, pose
us so many problems? Wouldn't you have thought
that familiarity would resolve some of these day-
to-day issues? Or is it that very familiarity that
breeds . . . whatever it breeds?

Does your mother know you're out?

In a world where ever greater numbers of women are going back to work after having children, the number of latchkey kids is growing. In 2002 a US Census report showed that 15 percent of children aged five to fourteen (some 5.8 million) spent at least six hours a week looking after themselves. That said, it is to be hoped that a caring mother not only knows that her child is out, but is either accompanying said child or has sent a note giving permission for the outing. Otherwise she could find social services knocking at her door in the very near future.

Do you want a smack?

Unlikely: only the truly masochistic enjoy being smacked. In the once-notorious Kinsey reports on sexual behavior (published in 1948 and 1953), the surprisingly high figures of 12 percent of females and 22 percent of males admitted to having an erotic response to a sadomasochistic story, but who was turned on by the sadism and who by the masochism is not recorded. They should, however, be encouraged to meet.

What! Will these hands ne'er be clean?

If you are, say, a mechanic, a coal miner, a dyer, or a lifelong chain smoker, possibly ne'er. If not, try an antibacterial soap (many of which claim to kill 99.9 percent of known germs). The outcome for Lady Macbeth might have been very different had she heard of hand sanitizer (though perhaps not if she followed the trend suggested in a recent survey by Wirthlin Worldwide, which found that only 75 percent of American women and a miserly 58 percent of men washed their hands after using public toilets).

Were you born in a barn?

Few people are, though Christian tradition has it that Jesus was born in a stable. Abraham Lincoln was born in a log cabin, as, allegedly, were six other US presidents—Andrew Jackson, Zachary Taylor, Millard Fillmore, James Buchanan, Ulysses S. Grant, and James Garfield—but for some reason it is Abe whose origins hit the headlines. The first Duke of Wellington, who was born in Ireland, once confounded a person who suggested he was Irish with the words, "Because a man is born in a stable, that does not make him a horse." It doesn't make him the Messiah, either . . . There is a school of thought that says this question was originally "Were you born in Bardney?" but as Bardney is a small village in the English county of Lincolnshire, with a population of 1,643 according to the last census, chances are you weren't born there either.

Who can find a virtuous woman? for her price is far above rubies

An unmounted Burmese (i.e., best-quality) cushion-cut ruby of 2.33 carats is offered at a price of US $22,500 per carat, or $52,425 in total. A 54 kg (119-pound) woman weighs 269,807 carats, and her minimum price, therefore, is $6,072,468. So to be valued "far above rubies," her price would be at least $6.5m, I'd say. And that's before running costs, depreciation, fair wear and tear, etc. . . . In terms of rarity, if you are referring to the virtuous woman of Proverbs 31:10 (i.e., good at housework, chaste, God-fearing, wise, yada-yada . . .) you'll be hard pushed to find her this side of the Promised Land.

When I play with my cat, who knows whether she isn't amusing herself with me more than I am with her?

A surprisingly foolish question considering its begetter, the French philosopher Michel de Montaigne—normally a rock-solid source of common sense. Montaigne himself is admitting that he doesn't know the answer, and you can be perfectly certain that the cat doesn't. An approximation of what the cat is thinking would be "Googoo-bleh!" It is only cat obsessives who insist that the animals are intellectual giants. The average cat has a brain taking up just 0.9 percent of its total body mass (a human's takes up 2 percent) and its cerebral cortex is about $1/35$ of a human's. OK, so a cat might be able to work out how to use a cat-flap and can spot the cat-hater in a room full of feline fanatics in no time at all. But have you ever seen one open a can of food? Use a set of keys to get through the door like everybody else? Finish a crossword? No, I thought not.

In fact, a philosopher who believes that a cat is capable of any intellectual activity as complex and abstruse as thought probably ought to consider changing career. To taxidermy, for instance.

Am I talking to myself?

If you are a parent or teacher, yes, you might as well be talking to yourself. The kids aren't listening, or if they are they aren't taking any notice. As a basic rule, a child's attention span should be about two to three minutes for every year of their age. So if you've been going on a while, your words are almost certainly falling on deaf ears. Furthermore, in 2006 the Center for Disease Control and Prevention estimated that 4.5 million American children aged five to seventeen have been diagnosed with attention-deficit hyperactivity disorder (ADHD). That's between 3 and 7 percent of school-aged children. So the statistics really are against you.

But you must have realized that, or you wouldn't have asked the question. So save your breath or be content with being your own audience. In a US online survey in 2010, from a sample of almost 1,500 people, 33 percent said they talked to themselves frequently and 51 percent did so occasionally. Only 3 percent said they never did. So you're not doing anything out of the ordinary.

Look at my face, does it look like I care?

Clearly not. You don't look as though you are at all bothered. Least of all about your grammar.

However, on occasions the person asking this question may be doing so to take attention away from the fact that they care very much. There aren't many of us who can completely control the subconscious expressiveness of our faces. So if the questioner is avoiding eye contact with you, displaying a sneer, or even crying buckets, you may assume that, "Yes, it rather looks as if you do care after all." Although you should bear in mind that your ability to read these nonverbal prompts might be undermined should your interlocutor has Botox-ed all the natural expression from his or her mug.

What do you think you are doing?

Something you shouldn't be. Just stop it. Now.

Actually, all of us find ourselves doing things unconsciously sometimes. This may be an action as simple as flicking our hair or biting our nails. However, we might also undertake rather more significant actions when we are in an altered state of mind and cannot call upon our normal thought processes. Some of these might be constructive—giving up smoking under hypnosis, for example. But they might also be destructive—for instance, if we are under the influence of alcohol or drugs. A few unfortunate people do quite terrible things when simply asleep. In Britain in November 2009, a man described as a "devoted husband" was acquitted of killing his wife while they both slept in a camper van. Suffering a sleep disorder, the defendant displayed "noninsane automatism" when he killed her while dreaming she was a male intruder.

What (sort of) time do you call this?

Later than it should be, obviously. You have either overslept and arrived at work halfway through a meeting, failed to meet your parents' curfew on a Friday night, or nipped out to the pub after work for a quick one, only to stagger home at closing time to find your dinner is in the dog.

CHAPTER EIGHT

Where's the beef?

Questions of food and drink

Isn't it remarkable how many questions about food and drink focus on the pros and cons of overindulgence? And why is it that no one has anything interesting to ask about water?

Dost thou think, because thou art virtuous, there shall be no more cakes and ale?

Quite the reverse is true: if thou art virtuous there will be more cakes and ale for the rest of us. So please feel free to be as virtuous as thou wilt and give me thy last Rolo. It was Sir Toby Belch in Shakespeare's *Twelfth Night* who first asked this question. He wouldn't have known—or cared—that on any given day, an estimated half of the American female population is on a diet, as opposed to one in four men, while UK statistics suggest some 37 percent of women and 18 percent of men are dieting most of the time. If Sir Toby was alive today, he would not have been one of them. He may have been fat, but he was happy. And drunk.

What shall we do with a drunken sailor?

Until 1970, we put up with him—indeed, if he was in the Royal Navy we encouraged him, because for almost 250 years we gave him a ration of rum every day and double before a battle; at one time the daily allowance was an extraordinary half a pint (600ml). How Britain came to be the world's greatest naval power when everyone who boarded a ship in her name was perpetually plastered is a question that the history books tend to sweep under the carpet (or perhaps over the yardarm). Nowadays, sailors have more of an incentive to remain sober: being drunk in charge of a boat is legally comparable to being drunk in charge of a car, so a drunken sailor may find himself paying a heavy fine or having his licence taken away.

Is it progress if a cannibal uses a knife and fork?

It could well be, if you go along with the English sexologist Havelock Ellis (1859–1939). He wrote that "what we call 'progress' is the exchange of one nuisance for another nuisance," and cutlery-wielding cannibals may have come to this conclusion when they realized that their fingers didn't get so dirty but they had to do more washing up.

While there continue to be odd reports of ritual cannibalism in certain corners of the world, it is thankfully a pretty rare phenomenon these days. This has less to do with the advent of knives and forks than with the power wielded in the eighteenth, nineteenth, and twentieth centuries by expansionist Western Christian nations in Africa, the Americas, and the Pacific. While this might be criticized on the one hand as unacceptable social imperialism, it was something of a boon for all those people who might otherwise have ended up as someone else's main course.

Or perhaps its popularity declined after the story spread of the two cannibals who ate a clown. The first asked the other: "What did you think?" The second replied: "Tasted funny." Boom boom.

Who ate all the pies?

Find the fattest person in the room (they won't be able to hide). It was probably them. This question is particularly apt if you are attending the annual World Pie-Eating Championship, held in Wigan in the north of England. With competitors taking on 5-inch-wide meat and potato pies (or slightly smaller vegetable versions for the non-meaties), until 2006 the winner was the person who ate the most pies over a set time. In 1998, Scott Ormrod managed a mighty eleven in 30 minutes. But then the health-and-safety brigade stepped in and today the challenge is to eat one pie more quickly than anyone else. In 2009 Barry Rigby won in 45 seconds. Impressive, yes, but what a spectacle might he have provided over half an hour?

Where's the beef?

It depends where you are: in the average supermarket, there is a clearly labeled "Meat" section offering beef of various cuts and kinds; in a vegetarian restaurant you may search in vain and have to settle for the spinach and ricotta quiche. Incidentally, the country exporting the most beef is Brazil, so the answer might also be: "On a ship coming out of Rio."

How many beans make five?

Five. Next question.

Fill all the glasses there, for why/
Should every creature drink but I?/
Why, man of morals, tell me why?

No reason at all, pal. The drinks are on you.

Have you ever seen a straight banana?

Probably not, but if you live in the European Community you won't have seen a very bendy one either. EC regulation 2257/94 requires that bananas be "free from malformation or abnormal curvature." With "Extra class" bananas, no deviation from this rule is permitted, though Class 1 bananas can have "slight defects of shape" and Class 2 bananas can have full-on "defects of shape." Bizarrely, given this amount of attention to detail, there is no definition of "abnormal curvature." Not in the case of bananas, that is. But someone *has* gone to the trouble of defining the permitted bendiness of cucumbers: Class I and "Extra class" cucumbers are allowed a bend of 10mm per 10cm of length, Class II twice as much. Those people in Brussels whose job it is to care about this sort of thing earn every penny of their salaries, don't they?

CHAPTER NINE

Will you still love me tomorrow?

Questions of sex and romance

What is it about love that turns us into nervous wrecks? Why do most of the questions in this chapter reveal deep-seated anxiety? Shouldn't love be a source of happiness, not misery? A somber note on which to end, perhaps, but what can you do?

Where is love?

It depends on whom you ask, but songwriters in particular have often found love in the strangest places. The Troggs and later Wet, Wet, Wet felt it in their fingers and toes (which some would say was remarkably chaste of them); others have maintained that it is in your eyes, in the air, even—though this is a bit of a cop-out—everywhere. The song from the musical *Oliver!* wonders if it might fall from skies above or lurk underneath an apple tree. But as it also manages to extract five syllables from that brief opening word, its views—like its pronunciation—might be considered a bit of a stretch.

For a more scientific explanation of where love is, it is worth speaking to neurologists. A team of scientists from University College London led by Andreas Bartels and Semir Zeki have in recent years identified four zones of the brain they believe are responsible for generating feelings of being "head over heels in love." By scanning the brains of people looking at images of their loved ones, they discovered all displayed heightened activity in specific parts of the brain (the medial insula and anterior cinguate of the cortex and deep in the striatum, since you ask) while the "switches" went off in those parts of the prefrontal cortex responsible for depression.

It might also be worth checking that the person posing the question is not simply looking for one of the six towns called Love in the USA.

Who wrote the Book of Love?

According to a medieval sect called the Cathars, Christ did: the "Book of Love" is a supposed gospel written in His own hand. Its teaching ran contrary to that of the Church, however, so the Cathars were much persecuted. Interesting that they should have gone down in history as heretics because they believed something that was alleged to come straight from the Son of God, but that's the medieval church for you.

How do I love thee?

The only way to deal with this is to dig out a poetry anthology and—as Elizabeth Barrett Browning suggests—count the ways. Even with this straightforward approach, however, the answer is "It depends." In her poem there are seven clear-cut ways, most of them pretty extravagant—"I love thee to the depth and breadth and height my soul can reach" is typical. The problem comes with the ending, when she says that "if God choose, I shall but love thee better after death." Elizabeth died in 1861, but posthumous reports about the state of her love remain thin on the ground. So the answer is either seven or eight, depending on whether or not you want to make a bet on God's view of the matter.

More recently, two California sociologists, Thomas Lasswell and Terry Hatkoff, have created a scale of different types of love. It includes: Romantic love; Best friend or companionate love; Unselfish love; Logical love; and Game-playing love. As can be seen, that only stretches to five types, which suggests a period of love deflation since the days of Elizabeth Barrett Browning. Disappointing.

How *you* doin'?

Many people make the mistake of thinking that this is a question, when in fact it is simply a salutation, meaning little more than "Hi!" Like "How do you do?" (see page 92) it neither seeks nor requires an answer. As used by Joey in the TV series *Friends*, however, it acquired the more specific meaning of "I should like to go to bed with you." The answer "OK" was assumed.

Who loves ya, baby?

As with the previous entry, this isn't a question—it means little more than "How about that?" or "Whaddya know?" (see *What's up, Doc?* on page 97, for a similar verbal "filler"). It was the catchphrase of Kojak, a shaven-headed cop played by Telly Savalas in the 1970s TV series of the same name. Popular worldwide, the show was dubbed into German with the title *The Lion Without a Mane*. Who says the Germans don't have a sense of humor?

Kojak was a snappy dresser who licked lollipops, wore tinted glasses indoors, and addressed people as "pussycat." In New York? In those days? Why wasn't he knifed before the end of Episode One? Because that combination of unlikely affectations made him supercool, that's why. The '70s, eh? I guess you had to be there.

What's new, Pussycat?

If you're talking to the cat you either live alone or you're a cat obsessive who insists your pet understands you, or both (see *When I play with my cat . . .* , page 119). I am certain your feline friend has little to disclose by way of headline-grabbing scoops. More likely it's deciding whether it's time to lick its ass again.

That is not to say that there aren't plenty of innovations in the cat (and cat accessories) market, though most seem designed to satisfy the yearnings of humans rather than Tibbles himself. Take, for instance, the emergence of specially bred hypoallergenic cats for those who suffer allergic reactions to fur. At almost $4,000 a pop, clearly they appeal to some people, though I suspect they are the sort who will instantly swap their allergy to cat hair for something else (nuts, gluten, celery, air . . . take your pick). Or for those who don't wish to deal with the natural detritus of their moggy, how about the self-cleaning litter box? Cat hoodies? Swarovski-encrusted collars? All new, Pussycat, and all, quite frankly, rather ridiculous.

In the film of this title the expression is to some extent analogous with Joey Tribbiani's "How *you* doin'?" (see page 140). The film's hit song, penned by Burt Bacharach and Hal David and recorded by Tom Jones, was nominated for an Oscar. Whoa, whoa, as you might say.

Was this the face that launched a thousand ships?

Of course not. Faces don't launch ships. Women with bottles of champagne launch ships. And even if she had had a thousand bottles of champagne, Helen of Troy—to whose face this question originally referred—couldn't have launched the Greek fleet, because she was in Troy at the time. Faust was in the throes of selling his soul to the Devil when he asked it, which may explain why his geography had gone a bit shaky.

Oi, Faust, she's over here.

Who ever loved that loved not at first sight?

Elizabeth and Darcy in *Pride and Prejudice*? Beatrice and Benedick in *Much Ado About Nothing*? Literature is full of couples who spend most of the book or play apparently hating each other before coming round to a different point of view. It's called dramatic tension. Interestingly, though, the idea of love at first sight remains a highly attractive one even in our modern world of cynicism. In Daniel Evan Weiss's 2001 book, *100% American*, he reported that 57 percent of US women are firm believers in the romantic notion.

Can you read my mind?

Lois Lane asked Superman this in the 1978 film. We don't know the answer, but we do know that he could tell she was wearing pink underwear, so there may be a warning there, girls: if you're contemplating dating a superhero, secrets (even if they are Victoria's) are going to be a thing of the past.

On a (slightly) more grounded level, telepathy—the unexplained transfer of thoughts or feelings directly from one mind to another—has long split the world into believers and nonbelievers. Part of the problem is that there is yet to be any widely accepted scientifically measurable proof of the phenomenon. However, Dean Radin, president of the Parapsychological Association, has argued that an overview of the results of large numbers of telepathic studies offers statistically significant evidence of its existence. Others—including the likes of Derren Brown, who has built a career on seemingly being able to read and manipulate others' thoughts—maintain that there is always a psychological rather than a paranormal explanation.

In 2006 biologist Dr. Rupert Sheldrake published a study revealing that people can accurately predict who is ringing them 45 percent of the time (and not just because the caller's name appears on their cell phone screen). He argues that this level of success rules out pure chance and suggests some sort of "telephone telepathy." Part-funded by Cambridge University's Trinity College, his findings nonetheless left many other scientists cold.

Could it be magic?

If it's David Blaine starving himself in a tank over the River Thames or David Copperfield making the Statue of Liberty disappear, it's probably not magic, no. There are countless books and television shows (all featuring people who can expect a lifelong ban from the Magic Circle for revealing trade secrets) explaining just how tricks such as these are done—and the answer is never very magical.

But if it's anything to do with an attraction to Barry Manilow (who sang a hit song with this title) there may well be some sort of spell involved. There's no other obvious explanation.

O what can ail thee, knight-at-arms,/ Alone and palely loitering?

What ails him, poor soul, is that La Belle Dame Sans Merci has him in thrall, according to a poem by John Keats that is named after her. Who La Belle Dame Sans Merci is is a rather more difficult question and its answer depends on your interpretation of the poem. The most literal one suggests that she is a fairy spirit who works her way through men like the blonde in a film noir. The knight-at-arms has met her wandering through a meadow and gone off with her to her elfin grot (that's a cave, by the way; it was obviously a prettier word in 1821 than it is now), which is precisely the sort of thing that chat-room guidelines warn against these days. He ends up haggard and woebegone, and some would say he is lucky not to have come off any worse.

Why so pale and wan, fond lover?

Well, it's most likely lovesickness. The problem with this is that it makes us even less attractive to the person we are languishing after. Who presumably doesn't like us much to start with or we wouldn't need to be languishing. In a 2005 article for *The Psychologist*, Frank Tallis outlines several other symptoms of lovesickness, ranging from mania (or hypomania), depression, anorexia, stress, and obsessive-compulsive disorder to a dicky tummy, sleeplessness, dizziness, and confusion. Hardly likely to win back an uncertain heart, is it? As the friend in Sir John Suckling's lyric advises, it's time to admit defeat. He/she is just not that into you.

Who can I turn to . . .

. . . if you turn away? At the risk of sounding harsh, turning toward anyone who will give you the time of day is likely to be a better bet. Pursuing someone who has made it clear that they don't want you is a losing battle for you and deeply tedious for everyone who has to listen over and over again to a recitation of your woes. See the previous entry for confirmation of this.

What kind of fool am I . . .

. . . who never fell in love? An unusual kind of fool: it is falling in love, not refraining from it, that reduces most of us to total idiocy. In an online survey conducted in 2009 with some 9,300 respondents, around 10 percent said that they had never been in love. It was not recorded how many considered themselves foolish as a result.

Will you still love me tomorrow?

Probably not. Asking this question—and at the same time wondering if this is a lasting treasure or just a moment's pleasure, and whether you can believe the magic of your companion's sighs—is putting him under exactly the sort of pressure that will have him reaching for his underpants and saying, "Gotta go" sometime in the next fifteen minutes.

Rather than ask the question out loud, just keep in mind some statistics. The average couple that makes it to the altar has a 57 percent chance of notching up fifteen years of marriage. Not brilliant, perhaps, but realistic. After that point, those couples who have stayed together are likely to remain together until one or other departs this mortal coil. Them's the facts, but spending hours, days, months, and years agonizing over them is likely to shorten the odds against your other half wanting to stick around. Trying to make your time together a pleasure—rather than forcing him to pander to your neuroses—is surely a better option.

When will I see you again?

All too often, the answer is: "Not in the immediate future, darling. So don't sit by the phone." Indeed, a 2007 survey by condom manufacturers Durex reported that some 45 percent of respondents had enjoyed (or possibly endured) at least one one-night stand in the previous twelve months.

What becomes of the brokenhearted?

In an article for the tellingly named www.been-dumped
.com, Lena Madrona split the "heartbreak" process into
six stages:

- The Realization—things are looking shaky in your
  relationship.

- The ACTUAL Realization—the breakup.

- The Crappy Part—life seems like it has ended.

- The Rage—you feel bitterness against your ex.

- The Crush—you start to notice that there are,
  after all, other fish in the sea.

- Freedom!—your ex no longer dominates your
  thoughts and you can even see him/her without
  your stomach lurching.

In short, and at the risk of sounding unsympathetic, the brokenhearted get over it. They cry a lot, eat chocolate, and sooner or later meet somebody else. It is surprising how rarely the world comes to an end just because somebody ditches you.

What's love got to do with it?

Not much, if the biopic of Tina Turner is anything to go by. It'll end in tears. But if that is a bit gloomy for you, consider instead the results of a survey by the Canadian magazine *The Coast* in 2010. It revealed that of those in relationships, 23 percent considered themselves the "luckiest person on the planet" while another 38 percent were "happy." A mere 18 percent felt either "restless," "lost," or "trapped." That all rather suggests that love has quite a lot to do with happiness. Or as Sophocles put it: "One word frees us of all the weight and pain of life: that word is love."

Shall I never see a bachelor of threescore again?

It would be very surprising if you didn't. There's a lot more of them than there were when Shakespeare asked this question in *Much Ado About Nothing*. In both the UK and the US in 2008 (the most recent figures available at the time of writing) the number of marriages was the lowest since records began some 150 years ago. In England and Wales only 21.8 out of every thousand unmarried men aged sixteen or over married in the course of the year, down from 22.4 in 2007. In the US, 29.4 percent of men aged eighteen and over had never married. Both healthy trends if bachelors are what you want. Bear in mind, however, that a man's being a bachelor is no guarantee that he'll be "eligible."

AFTERWORD

Rhetoric was an integral part of a classical education, not only in Ancient Greek times but right up to the Middle Ages in much of Europe.

Nowadays you would study it at university if you were taking a philosophy course, but probably not come across it otherwise.

Yet with education systems changing as rapidly as they do, you might be tempted to ask the question—appropriately enough at this stage of the book—where do we go from here?